The Mums Are Filled With Melancholy

ashley jane

Copyright © 2018 **Ashley Jane**
Cover Art © 2018 **Nadiya Saara El-Sharkawy**
Editor: **Matt Shirley**

Ashley Jane - BreathWords
Alabama, USA
www.breathwords.com

All rights reserved. No part of this publication may be reproduced, distributed, or transmitted in any form or by any means, without prior written permission, unless for the purposes of reviewing.

Author's Note: This is a work of fiction. Locales and public names are sometimes used for atmospheric purposes. Any resemblance to actual people, living or dead, or to businesses, companies, events, institutions, or locales are completely coincidental.

The Mums are Filled with Melancholy/
Ashley Jane 1st Edition
ISBN 978-1-7325327-1-7

This book is dedicated to all the lost ones:
the bruised souls and the delicate hearts
just trying to find their way home.

You are not alone.

Contents

Foreword	5
Intention	9
Starve	51
War	91
Eclipse	131
Daybreak	169
Acknowledgements	207
About the Author	209
Contributors	213

Foreword

I was introduced to Ashley Jane and her poetry by our dear friend Alfa Holden, and I immediately fell in love with her unique ability to bring life to her art, something I look for in the words of any writer I read.

To say that Ashley Jane is a gifted writer would be far too easy, but it would be nothing less than the truth. She is a poet after my own heart and to read a few lines of her work is to be invited into her soul, taken to the core of her pain or the source of her pleasure, and connect with the imagery she paints so beautifully.

Ashley holds nothing back when she writes, placing her very soul on display in the pages of 'The Mums are Filled with Melancholy', and she does so while never attempting to stray from her authentic voice.

It is a gift to write poetry as well as Ashley has in this book, and oh, how she made it look easy, but I know with complete certainty that

Ashley's talent is not only anything but easy, it's bursting with that spark, that thing that burns in every poet worth their salt when they release it on the page. All great writers and poets possess this gift to some degree, but Ashley Jane has it in spades.

To read this book is to feel like finally coming home again, like someone out there knows your deepest secrets and sacred truths, and they still love you anyway. This book is a testament to Ashley's skill as a writer, her beautiful creativity, and her passion to overcome any obstacle life chooses to throw at her. Ashley's passion is here, and here is a good place to be.

- Nicole Lyons, author of Blossom and Bone

The Mums Are Filled With Melancholy

Someone once told me
that I write too much s a d poetry,
all melancholy
and soul-aching

(I wear mums as window dressing)

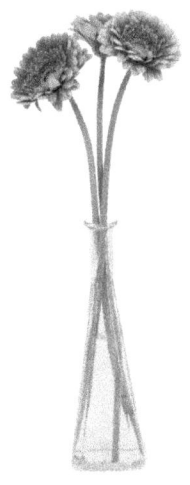

ashley jane

The Mums Are Filled With Melancholy

*"Heartache wasn't my intention
...love was"*

- Alfa

His kiss
tasted different now,
like the
beginning
of
goodbye

(his lips were filled with leaving)

The Mums Are Filled With Melancholy

I'm not sleeping well these days
my mind is silently screaming,
and I've tucked my heart away
(it violently shudders in the corner)

my fragile lungs are choking on fear
while my soul is stitched in memories
that make it far too hard to breathe

(*I need to rip out the remnants of you here*)

I dug out our old pictures,
snapshots I had tucked away in shoeboxes
and saved
as if waiting
for you to come back and reminisce

the past has been tugging at me,
offering up an invitation
to revisit all those memories
that I shouldn't miss,
that I try to forget

I wanted so much
to leave these reminders in ashes,
burn the photos
and walk away with a clean slate

yet, here I am,
surrounded by a legacy
of moments better left buried

(an inheritance of photographic agonies)

I'll call today
HEARTACHE
because it's pressing on my chest,
and I'm out of breath

(*this sorrow leaves me gasping*)

I think

I loved you most at 3am
when you'd tune
your old acoustic guitar
and write songs about a life
neither of us had lived yet

we were miles apart, but
under the same cherry moon
we enjoyed pretending
that we were immortal,
that we had forever

in reality,
we were already over
long before we were bathed
in its light

we thought
we could capture happiness
in polaroids
and letters
and late night talks,
live as if this wasn't some
short-term tryst with fantasy

The Mums Are Filled With Melancholy

I knew it was dangerous,
this thing we were doing,

especially the part
where I gave you my heart

then again,
I was always fine with taking risks
with my own

in the end,
it was yours
I wasn't willing to risk

(*it was a chance I couldn't take*)

ashley jane

we were temporary,
a strawberry spring,
pastels and petals blooming just to deceive,
wishes and wings beating
inside fragile hearts,
a glimpse of paradise before falling apart

(we were all flicker and fade)

The Mums Are Filled With Melancholy

this wind carries words
whispered over distances
that we refuse to cross

(*each breeze kisses my skin with goodbyes*)

ashley jane

we ran hot and cold,
wild fire tempered by frost
we were never very good
at finding middle ground,
too determined to push against the pull

you taught me that love
always comes in extremes,
and now I'm left craving the
BLAZING, BITING BURN

(*this fire is a powerful addiction*)

The Mums Are Filled With Melancholy

we were a love
that stormed the beaches
and crashed against the shore
like powerful waves,
the spring breeze and summer heat

we were
a wrecking ball
of fire and flame,
untouchable
in our pursuit
of destruction

but, we were
seasonal
and seasons turn,
the heat
of August fades
with the snow
of December,
the sandy shore no longer warm
as it's washed out to sea

(*everything comes to an end*)

summer
never tasted
quite the same after you,
too saccharine sweet
and filled with uncertainty,

and I was left craving
a different kind of sugar

(and a different kind of heat)

bittersweet moments
tossed aside
for clean sheets,
all soft white and empty

(*I'm tired of getting lost in your memories*)

tell me again

about how I was born of the sea
and how all the waves
now carry the crash of my name

tell me how my eyes
sparkle bolder than the moon,
how they are like turquoise stars
and how without me,
the night sky
just isn't bright enough anymore

tell me again
how the mysteries of the world
can't hold a candle
to the mysteries
that linger
beneath my skin

tell me how you want
to discover them
one
by
one

The Mums Are Filled With Melancholy

tell me again
how you kept all those poems I wrote,
and how you tucked them
in a reliquary
because they were the closest to holy
that you've ever been

now, tell me how you forgot all of it
because I keep trying

(I can't seem to purge you from my veins)

I planted beauty,
waited for it to grow,
flowers and moss
to match your emerald eyes

but, you watered the petals with pretty lies,
turned dandelion dreams
into thorns of betrayal,
and left fields of trust
overgrown with weeds

now, there is nothing left to bloom,
and the ghosts in the garden
all look like you

(your spirit haunts the snowdrops)

ashley jane

you asked me for the time
and wanted to know about the weather
and all I could think about was the year
when winter stripped away
the last pieces of us

(I'm barely holding on,
and you barely remember)

we were so busy putting out fires
that we let our own die out
I recall those cold nights
and feeling like I'd never get warm
the front yard was drowning
in carnations and frost,
and I was lost in memories of us
unable to come up for air

(*I finally surfaced in spring*)

I stalled out somewhere
along your highway of broken dreams,
detoured through
the fog of forgotten memories,
battled the barriers
around your bonfire heart,
got lost on the journey
trying to find your soul,
barely breaking away before it all fell apart

(you were a map filled with chaos)

I let you carve your name
onto my heart,
let you etch your face
into my dreams

you became permanent,
a soul deep tattoo
that left me hovering
between heaven and hell

and now this ache is all that's left,
bruised and broken moments
imprinted in my mind,
shoebox memories that I can't hide,
and the sting of knowing
that I'll never rid myself of you

(I should've used washable ink)

ashley jane

I felt the love leave,
a
V I O L E N T
uprising

now, only emptiness remains

I thought you said
you'd always care

(your 'always' had an expiration date)

the clocks are broken
and the stars are gone
and my hands are too cold
without yours to hold

time is just a series of sleepless nights,
insomnia leaving me
emotionally anesthetized

my mind focuses on the minute hand
while I'm slowly forgetting
the taste of your kiss

(*I'm still waiting to make my wish*)

it's 3am

the candlelight flickers,
foreboding,
foretelling,
all those steps forward
and yet, here we are
stumbling backwards
in the dark
—

you paint my champagne heart
in shades of shadows
just don't let the shimmer
fade to black
(there is no going back)
—

I'm right
— *I am, right?* —
and it's alright
I know eventually
the ache will subside
we suffer through the torture
of a long goodbye
with no reason why

(but it's time)

the written words

on the screen,
a hushed goodbye
said so eloquently
and delicately
as if I were going to break
upon reading it

the walk away,
feet carefully placed
with steps in stride
as you hurry along
hoping that I don't
stand up and
beg you to return

the fragile silence
that follows,
an aching reminder
of an attempt to reach out
that failed
because people
with hearts like yours
never learned how
to put down roots

(your soul wasn't made for staying)

I spilled emotion
on the page
that didn't belong to you,
but you claimed it
for your own

(not everything is about you

...but this one is)

The Mums Are Filled With Melancholy

You sent lilies
(my favorite)
in a plea for forgiveness,
but I hate when flowers
are used as an apology

(nature isn't an 'I'm sorry')

bruises
and broken dreams

memories that
linger and pause
in different hues

sadness betrayed
by the most beautiful
shades of blue

and we keep looking
for someone to blame

destiny
chance
fate

or whatever the hell else
we choose to call it

because
if we admitted the truth,
that we saw the end
rushing up to meet us

that we foretold
the collapse
and did nothing
to try and change it

well,
then we'd also have to admit
that this whole mess
was our own damn fault

(we were never good at accepting blame)

ashley jane

I got caught up
in your sights and sounds,
in your pretty words and promises

I became blinded by your light
and, you left me *FLOUNDERING,*

lost in moments I couldn't escape
you want me to forgive and forget

(but, I can't forgive and I won't forget)

The Mums Are Filled With Melancholy

I listened to too many love songs,
and I held you a little too close
I hoped you'd let me call you sweetheart
(cause that's what lovers do, right?)

we played the part perfectly,
two hopeless romantics,
singing along to wind songs,
two lights, twin flames,
keeping us warm each night

but, it all became so overwhelming,
your love hanging on to my depression
and, no two flames are really the same

(*no love song ever tells you that*)

we keep trying
to mend this gap between us,
hoping that today won't be more of the same
(the silence weighs heavy here)
but we were always better at burning bridges
than we were at repairing them

(the path back now lies in smoke)

I wasn't sure
if you would answer
heaven knows,
we were never very good at keeping in touch

(I suppose that miles
aren't the only kind of distance between us)

I just wanted you to know –
I still remember
all those late nights
and how you taught me to love myself

(*I hope you're doing well*)

I flew through your fires
on cranes of peace,
painted your darkness with a lavender skyline

I carried your pain like a beast of burden,
taking the tremble of your soul
and making it my own

and you said my heart wasn't like the others,
that it was too soft, too fragile
for such a vicious world,
and then you showed me exactly
how love hurt

I may have scars now,
but you were wrong
and you should've known

(*my heart was always strong*)

my soul
was calling out your name again,
aching to reminisce,
while aquamarine waves
crashed inside my ocean heart,
keeping me awake

they asked that I write you,
told me to put the letter in a bottle,
and they would deliver it
to our place on the shore

(but you don't live there anymore)

ashley jane

we only survive in passing glances,
our whispered words fading
we've become nothing more
than two souls in waiting,
longing for a time and place,
a sanctuary that no longer exists

we drift in and out,
colliding with the pressing silence
and the deep ache we feel within

we've become lost along the way,
like hometown strangers
with no place to call home

(*hiraeth*)

The Mums Are Filled With Melancholy

we are nothing more than faces
in old photographs,
vintage mementos dipped in black and white
we are faraway places
etched with the longitudes of time,
memories dimming with each sunrise,
color fading quickly,
ruined by the light,
until distant hearts
are all that remain

(*wistful whispers carefully engraved*)

ashley jane

we became distant
neither friend nor foe,
just hearts entwined
with indifference
and the ability
to accept this fate

(*we turned love into apathy*)

The Mums Are Filled With Melancholy

these bones
are made with
the ashes
of all those past
loves

(*I am darkness and dust*)

some days,
I believe you were just a dream,
my subconscious's creation,
a figment of my own imagination

but, the ghost of you
still lingers
in dark corners
and jagged edges

and, I am still running
from all those shadows
you left behind

(I'll never truly be rid of you)

from the moment
we met,
I was so caught up
in your orbit
that I assumed the stars
shined only for you

gravity has
a way of pulling us back down,
of spinning into the black,
and it left me afraid
that I'd never
see them shine
like that anymore

yet here they are,
showing me
that change
isn't always
a bad thing

the stars still shine,
just a little differently now

(I still get lost in them)

ashley jane

"*do birds go hungry
awaiting a storm its break,
will i too here shrivel?*"

-Emma Blas

ashley jane

we float,
prayers on a river stream
that is spilling out
into a chrysanthemum sea
we whisper incantations to the moon,
invoke the ghosts in the frothy waves
we keep close to the surface,
hovering
like a silent fog rolling in,
drifting through the seasons
of life
and love
of dark
and death

(*we sink*)

slow stutter start,
mind clogged mental stop,
and these thoughts burn
a dark hole in me,
aphasia ache denying words release

(*they call it writer's block*)

I've forgotten how the light looks,
the one that used to run through my veins,
the one now bandaged up
behind the darkest clouds
(HIDING IS A HABIT THAT'S SO HARD TO BREAK)

and I can feel myself withdrawing
I've gotten really good at running away,
vacancy signs in these distant eyes
(I KNOW I PROMISED THAT I WOULD CHANGE)

now I'm hoping
if I pour my thoughts out here in the dark,
these words will illuminate
my shadowed heart
(I need these wounds to HEAL,
so it's a chance I have to take)

(*abience*)

seeds of doubt rest
amid rambling thoughts

wavering back and forth
over every decision,
a constant stream
of information

as whispers of anxiety
take up residence

(*renting out my wavering mind*)

the emptiness
within
took her breath away,

like a
nothingness
inhaled into
lungs that wouldn't work

there is panic in her eyes,
and air comes in frantic gasps
while her heart beats too fast
within its bone cage

she is spilling roses
while drowning in pain

all those pretty petals
falling to the floor
as she sheds a mask
that doesn't hide her
anymore

she suffocates on the raw
and the real,
on the aching wounds
that just won't heal

The Mums Are Filled With Melancholy

until
the wasteland of words in her throat
finally
free
fall
from her lips

(see the beautiful poetry raining down)

The Mums Are Filled With Melancholy

blackened petals
falling silently
in the pristine chill,
a stark contrast
against nature's
white innocence,
a flawless dark
so reminiscent
of her heart,
burned and broken,
ruined to the core,
with pieces dropping,
waiting for the
cold rush of air
to blow them
far away from here

(more charred remains scattered in the wind)

ashley jane

she is inside herself again,
holding hands with her depression,
tied in tangles with talking ghosts,

but, there is a little piece of her hanging on,

knowing the madness
will set her free

(*maybe, it'll set me free too*)

The Mums Are Filled With Melancholy

echoes of sorrow
pierce the blackest of nights
she sits
 - a little ruined, a little lost -
all those dreams STOLEN
while she clings
to hope on a string
but it never really means anything
just another rope tethered to the shadows,
and she doesn't know
how to let go

(I'm not sure how to let go either)

ashley jane

I was tangled up,
tied in complex knots
of melancholy
and dark dreams,
waiting for someone
to see shapes
in this muddled mess
waiting for anyone to see
that I stood
a little too close to the edge,
waiting and wavering,
so torn between
wanting to survive
and wondering
if anyone would notice
my fall

(*thank you for noticing*)

The Mums Are Filled With Melancholy

all these memories are building up,
creating a tower
that will inevitably tumble down
and here I am,
fighting the urge
to drown in the debris

(*but, these walls won't rebuild themselves*)

ashley jane

she blooms disillusioned,
pulled petals floating through the air
on hollow wings,
a windfall of sadness
chased with whiskey's sting

she is wilting innocence and naïveté,
no longer fooled by magic or fortune or fate

she now blossoms in the darkness,
a flowering ghost, lost and broken,
her beauty exiled to the place
where only silence is spoken

(you'll find her in the shadows)

The Mums Are Filled With Melancholy

you can feel
the melancholy sadness
in each teardrop
that rolls down
her cheek,
in the coldness
that sits against her skin,
in each shuddered breath
she takes in
you can feel it in each word
she doesn't say

it all hangs in the silence,
begging to be heard

(are you listening)

ashley jane

she has locked herself away,
bound herself to a home
with far too many skeletons
lurking in the shadows,
too many wandering steps
that lead nowhere,
dark forest hallways
and melancholy mazes

she herself is a haunted house,
a subconscious filled
with lonely rooms
that echo in the emptiness,
a dark angel lost in her own mind,
waiting on someone
to come find her

(*beware the ghost*)

The Mums Are Filled With Melancholy

these gray days leave me aching
while nights find me drowning in sorrow
I am endless bits and pieces
tangled and twisted by crashing waves
and there is no empathy in these seas,
no reprieve in their dark depths
this sinking heart of mine is an anchor

(and it's weighing me down)

ashley jane

you speak to me in dark dreams,
but my mind doesn't like the quiet
and my soul doesn't like to sleep

(*too many ghosts live in the silence*)

the mums are bleeding
and there are secrets in the reeds
and the air is heavy,
clammy from the press
of lingering goodbyes

sweet morning memories
now taste like aching nights
filled with too many things
we'll always remember
and too many things
we'd do anything to forget

(each petal is a reminder)

frost settles in a little too close
the night is crying blankets of white,
and I am lost in this ineffable sadness,
its ice biting cold
sinking into every curve of my bones,
solitude and sorrow etched in deep,
and the heat of the day seems too far away
to thaw my aching heart

(*I just need a little warmth*)

The Mums Are Filled With Melancholy

she is slowly
S
  I
    N
K
  I
  N
G
under,
searching for the strength
to get her through,
mind clouded with doubts
and darkness,
heart tight in her chest
as she struggles
to reach the surface,
her tired body
weighing her down

(the shadows watch her drown)

she is saying goodbye,
her thoughts becoming irrelevant
she fades into the background

she is late nights under street lights
that startle and stun,
a sacred silence beside a fractured horizon

she is saying goodbye,
her thoughts becoming irrelevant
she fades into the background

her words have fallen like poison rain
slowly corroding and eating away
at a faithless heart
that no longer beats steady
her mind is heavy,
and her legs are unstable
as she clings to memories
on melancholy chords

she is saying goodbye,
her thoughts becoming irrelevant
she fades into the background

(just another ghost of the city)

she likes
the feeling
of falling,

slip sliding
into shadows
to explore
what lies beneath,

sucked into zero gravity
as she tries to uncover
what lurks in your mind,
all those dark places
you've left behind

she wants to discover you,
to plummet headlong
into your destruction,
to understand what makes you tick,
to find out what happened
to your innocence

(*so maybe, she can find her own again*)

ashley jane

she pens moments of melancholy,
tears writing letters
for her future self to read,
ink-stained art from the heart
filled with blood and memories

(*signed, sealed, delivered*)

blue
runs through my mind
all the time
like a spiral
spinning downwards
into a melancholy I can't prevent

and I am drowning in it

this deluge of doubts,
swimming in this anxious misery
that blooms within my chest,
the aching press
of dark clouds and gray skies

there is no peace amidst depression,
no hope in the acknowledgement
that time looms on

(*I keep reminding myself to stay strong*)

she floats

outside herself,
her mind slightly fractured
by the sound of her screaming heart

she heals the ache
by conjuring an escape,
fabricating a dream-state,
a fantasy
beyond the realms
of reality

she hemorrhages emotions,
staining the page
with warring thoughts,
the back and forth
eating away at her soul

she is aware,
but not really there,
a flickering ghost
detached from her home

(her mind was never meant to be
a safe place to explore)

unrecognizable
just a distant figure
in a fading reflection

a mirror of ghosts
watching every move
while glass echoes
hollow words

you slowly walk away,
whispering goodbye
to the stranger
that you used to be

(*she doesn't exist anymore*)

mums
lined up like a funeral procession,
muted shades of a dying faith

I watch them placed
strategically around the room,
little beacons of memories in bloom

and I
have to hide in the hallway outside,
watching strangers cry in the corner

by tonight,
I'll have plucked every last petal
and woven them into a blanket of sadness
that smells just like you

(this is why I call them dead people flowers)

The Mums Are Filled With Melancholy

all rationality ceases,
reality divides,
sanity split apart

she's holding on
with a delicate grasp,
so overwhelmed
and constantly
cutting herself
on the jagged edges
and twisted corners,
slamming against
the wall of rocks

words flooding the paper
and getting washed away,
thoughts
that she's no longer
in control of
swept up in a torrent of cries,
trapped in a whirlpool of goodbyes

(*reason pulled out to sea*)

I'm fading again,
wisps of winter wrapping me up
in its slow moving cold,
moonlight shadows settling in to my soul,
a ghost in a shell slipping into the dark,
sorrow pressing heavy on an aching heart
the warm touch of summer has left my home
– the fire is gone

(*how do you expect me to hold on*)

eyes close
and the world goes dark,
no dreams or pictures or memories,
no lingering doubts rising up
from the shadows

(I wonder what it would be like…
to truly rest in peace)

I once bloomed

in limitless shades,
in delicate wisteria petals and tall oak trees,
in woodland magic and clover green
but, colors fade into languid grays,
a monochrome melancholy settling in
I am now motionless moments
and white noise

(I am a ghost in the wind)

The Mums Are Filled With Melancholy

I am shaky hands,
a racing heart and unsteady breaths
(THIS ANXIETY STEALS THE OXYGEN IT SEEMS)

I am suffocating on this feeling,
the heaviness, the ache, the dread it brings
(YOU WONDER WHY I WRITE? THIS IS WHY.)

there is something cathartic
about confession
there is medicine in spilling
my own poetic truth

(there is healing in this purge of words)

we cleanse the air
with incense and sage,
but this summertime
sadness lingers
long into fall

and we lie here awake,
drifting, restless,
our treasonous minds
creating an ache
that can't be seen

a heaviness that weighs
beneath flesh and bone,
gripping too tight,
making it
hard to breathe

(the doctor calls it dysthymia)

your heart is a ghost town
with its tangled web of hungry shadows,
its darkness cloaked in monsters
and your mind
is an abandoned forest
filled with nothing but an eerie quiet

it's suffocating, isn't it?
  all that pressing silence
  —
  I know how that feels

(*I've always been haunted*)

we dared destiny,
leaving little pieces of ourselves
scattered and intertwined,
so sure that fate
would never leave us broken

yet,
here
we are

numb,

fading,

and in
p i e c e s

(*we should've known better*)

somewhere
within my heart,
buried in a garden
of glass bones,
live shattered stories
that still hold
tendrils of magic
locked up tight
behind a frail rib cage

one day,
they'll find the key

(*one day, they'll break free*)

ashley jane

my mind awakens,
memories invading
the quiet moments

reminders lurking
in the shadows,

resurrected thoughts
haunting the day
while
flashes and figments
stalk the night

(*I'm not afraid of ghosts anymore*)

ashley jane

"*I wonder if I'll ever reach a point where I'm at peace or if I'll always be at war.*"

- Chelsea Lopez

ashley jane

sky above and sea below,
holding tight
to clouds and daydreams
as endless waves
crash against the shore
we stand on the edge
between the two,
eyes closed tight,
and with one breath,
we are tumbling forever more

(*watch us sink these memories*)

the sky is stained in shades
of violet, mint and roses,
and I am quietly drowning
in these emerald seas
(THE FIGHT IN MY FIRE FEELS LIKE IT IS DYING)

my once resilient heart
beats a little slower now,
searching out a tomb on the ocean floor

but, I can still hear
the calm within the chaos,
the wind's anxious whispers
guiding me back to shore

(what happens when they stop calling my name)

forever
once tasted like rainfall
and salty seas,
but this storm is filled
with stolen wishes
and these ocean wave promises
are made for breaking

(we crash against a melancholy shore)

The Mums Are Filled With Melancholy

we spent too much time
looking out the window,
alone in our own minds,
resting in solitude
with our own downpour of doubts

we became so good
at hiding the pain,
slow-dying smiles covering up
the ache that reigned

we let our worried minds
drown out our bleeding hearts,
so desperate for someone
or something
to save us
before the melancholy
tore us apart

(but, they never came)

stilled hearts,
aching to explore,
grounded by ghosts following far too close
and the tiny threads that bind us to them,
like little midnight stories of former glories
taking up residence in our bones

salt in the wound of a restless soul
that endeavors to be anywhere but home

(*we are restless*)

I wept
alongside a tearful moon,
listened to the stars
recite slow sonnets of the dark,
read stories secreted away,
once lost lines
now etched into the skies

they wax poetic
on beauty's demise
and the day
the sun fell from grace

(*I relate*)

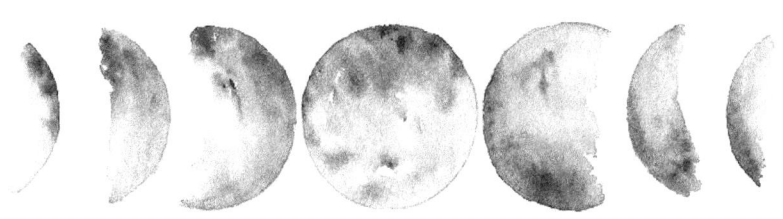

ashley jane

we bottled it all up,
the hurt, the sadness, the pain
we let it make a home inside us
for far too long
we tried to rid ourselves of it,
thinking that the waves would carry it away
but, it was too late

now, the sea is angry,
and all that pain
is a tsunami of rage

(it's battering down the door to our hearts)

we escape beneath the gentle waves,
lost somewhere between asleep and awake,
endless nights drifting on shifting currents,
moments of eternity slowly slipping away
(our broken hearts
      are drowning in memories)
we are breathless and boundless,
lissome longings sinking ocean deep,
restless souls searching across the sea

(we're aching for peace)

ashley jane

we are nights
spent remembering
everything...

...that we
spend all day
trying to forget

(*some things can't be forgotten*)

The Mums Are Filled With Melancholy

we are red dust
pouring from a bleeding earth,
our souls standing in suspended disbelief,
the weight of emptiness heavy on our backs

we are the midnight dreary,
hearts derailed by rhyme and ruin,
rights denied, but too tired to fight

we are unconsciously lost,
our minds spinning away from us
as we struggle to hold on

(fugue state)

ashley jane

we shelter our hearts with walls and wars,
fighting through the epic darkness,
hiding ourselves behind so many masks
that we forget who we are
we keep searching for reminders,
our spirits lingering
on cold, dark December nights
we float like ghosts through haunted halls,
our melancholy souls reaching out

(*the shadows will bring us together*)

The Mums Are Filled With Melancholy

time is fragile
hearts are fragile
we pretend we aren't,
but we are

we've got flower petals blooming
beneath our skin,
beauty planted deep within
—
orchids and irises
we are far too dark for roses
—
we water them with tears sometimes,
maybe even wrap our dark in softness,
I suppose it's fragile too

(*we won't admit it though*)

slow motion moments
hovering in the dark,
the faintest flicker of color
woven in-between the grays

(*we drown in melancholy seas*)

we were always best at running,
one breath from being swept away
we were tear drops and train tracks
without a need for looking back
we kept our damage under lock and key,
always looking over our shoulder,
watching as time loomed closer,
slow and painful and lonely
we lost ourselves in oak tree forests
and wild, restless fields,
places where our secrets could be kept
and our hearts would remain safe

(*we run because it's the only way*)

I met you
in a down pour
of lost souls
seeking shore,
where a mad melody
of crashing waves
reached up
to touch the rain
we were left struggling
to come up for air,
our hearts tight
and thoughts laid bare
as the clouds shouted
with a thunderous roar,
constantly pushing
and demanding more

(*we will not survive this storm*)

The Mums Are Filled With Melancholy

there are secrets imprinted
in these night skies,
whispers carried on the winds
of circling ravens
we are the solemn souls
trying to decipher them
while tangled up
in roses and thorns,
in magic and marigold,
our reticent hearts
beating in the dark,
listening to the call of the wild,
the prelude to an end,
this year of moonlight
destined to fade with the sun

(and us with it)

ashley jane

we lived on the cusp
of something great,
caught up
in the pleasant beauty
of the ocean waves

but even the waves
are pulled back
by the tide,
leaving us to crash,
pieces breaking up

we became
another casualty
of the ocean's rage,
like the reefs and wrecks,
left to wither and fade

(someone will discover us someday)

The Mums Are Filled With Melancholy

vintage memories
slowly f *l o a* t ɪɴ g
through the black and white

we muddle them together,
remembrance
in a million muted shades of gray

(*moments best left forgotten*)

we let them in

we open our hearts up to strangers, knowing that it'll only lead to destruction, to pain, to that sucker punch feeling. knowing they'll take pieces of us when they go. but, we do it anyway, because it's all we know how to do. and, because maybe, one day, we'll need a heart that opens its doors to us, too.

(just a thought)

The Mums Are Filled With Melancholy

the nights have become stagnant,
filled with reticence and tattered dreams

we wrote away the midnight stars
and tore hope at the seams

now, we are just spilled words
and wasted breaths,
our darkness destroying
all the light that was left

we barred the gates to the ever after,
filled the shadows with lavish disaster,
closed off all means of escape

we sit in the stillness

(*we drown in the ache*)

ashley jane

we find the sadness
amidst the city screams,
darkness personified in dead trees,
a bittersweet blight
causing colors to fade,
the bold beauty
now washed away

just like the flowers
that once bloomed in our hearts,
now left in the dark,
battered (but not broken)
a bit too close to falling apart

our cascading tears
water the falling leaves

we are a garden of sorrow
lost in a forest of catastrophes

(maybe autumn will remind us to breathe)

ashley jane

The Mums Are Filled With Melancholy

we were filled
with moments of infinite sadness,
trembling tears
falling from tangled webs
we cleansed our souls
under an autumn moon

(but, our hearts are still bound to winter)

ashley jane

we buried our ghosts beneath the waves,
trapped them in a deep ocean spell
that left us abruptly abandoned

we let their words sink to the sandy floor,
taking with them all the peace
we could never find

we watched our memories
get swept away
until no trace remained,
just the language of silence
echoing in the empty spaces

(but, there is no peace in this quiet)

we burn the dead reminders
that still linger
like aching pain and blood on our fingers
that we wash away under August showers
when the heat of day
collides with the cool night
we bury them in meadows of tall wheat grass
and dust our hands
of any remaining memories,
only to watch the remnants
rise before our eyes,
now a field flowing with forget-me-nots
and dandelions

(some things can't be burned)

we are hidden away,
kept secrets lost in the pages
of books no longer read

we are stored on shelves
that no one can reach,
tucked into dark corners,
our story not told
because who wants sad truths
when new fiction is fabricated
d a i l y

we are the forgotten ones,
our aches echoing through the quiet,
our hopes destroyed,
each chapter and verse burned
by apathy

(our words met only with silence)

The Mums Are Filled With Melancholy

we built a kingdom
from wilted petals
and let the ghosts
roam free

(we turned the mums into a home)

ashley jane

I am a collector of sad souls,
and shadows,
of faces painted with fake smiles
and hearts that want to drown
I watch them crash
like waves against the shoreline,
pretty pieces and parts
that were once whole,
now looking for a home

(I offer them my own)

The Mums Are Filled With Melancholy

thunderstruck
and lightning silenced,
we listen to the quiet,
to the ghosts who beckon
ONE LAST CALL FOR LOST SOULS,
all the captured hearts
with fractured parts
and no place to call home

    this is the sanctuary
    for the haunted,
    those with midnight eyes
    and melancholy in their bones

(you're no longer alone)

ashley jane

we spend too much time
in empty rooms,
too much energy on broken hearts,
and too much money trying to buy
a little piece of happiness
that will never last for long

(*less is more*)

The Mums Are Filled With Melancholy

we live in the shadows
where chaos is currency,
and melancholy is a commodity
that everyone owns
the days lay in ruins,
and we are too busy searching
for our own sense of self
to notice that the night will soon collapse

(*it'll take us with it*)

we watch the news
drone on and on,
skipping the
important things
because it makes life
PRETTIER

but, life isn't meant
to be pretty
or fair,
and God knows
it isn't meant to be easy

it is a complicated mess
of emotions,
and craziness,
and insanity

I am a complicated mess
of moments that sting
and memories that ache
and this press of sadness
that sits resolutely on my chest

we pretty things up
and pretend
that we don't struggle,
but life is a struggle

The Mums Are Filled With Melancholy

every day
without fail

we can hide behind
smiles and lies,
but, there is no use
in sugarcoating it
when we all know the truth

(we're all one step away from the edge)

I listened to the skies,
to the way the thunder would curse
and the clouds would cry

I fell in love with their song
and how they made sadness
sound so hauntingly beautiful

(melancholy makes such pretty music)

The Mums Are Filled With Melancholy

we are on the verge
of drowning,
the past rising up
in a torrent of feelings
and raining memories,
too many words pouring
from too many open wounds

we are a tidal wave of emotion
threatening to capsize
our rocking hearts
and wash us out to sea

but we'll never find closure
if we can't withstand the floods

(*bring on the rain*)

we left pieces of ourselves
on scraps of paper,
crumpled up moments
and memories categorized as mistakes
we spilled ourselves onto the page,
words written hastily and then tossed away

(sometimes, we just need to let it all out)

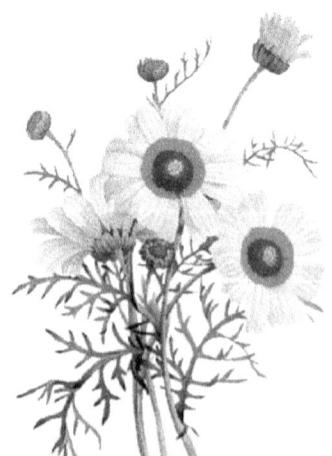

spilled confessions
leak from my veins,
formerly so
carefully hidden
beneath layers of
innocent lies,
all those thoughts
that rested dormant
under the surface,
words and worlds held back,
unable to breathe

But, now they are free:
words,
thoughts,
emotions,
unrestrained

(*I am uncontained*)

ashley jane

> *"I will enter your darkness
> to bring you light,
> to show you that even shadows
> are sacred and eclipsed by night"*

\- Gypsy Mercer

ashley jane

I *see your soul*
filled with dancing demons,
tattooed with tsunamis
meant to wash everyone away

you keep your heart closed away in a cage,
all the paths that once led there
now stitched up with loose ends

I know it gets lonely in all that silence

(*please, let me in*)

The Mums Are Filled With Melancholy

we both used to glimmer,
all diamonds and daisies and daffodil dreams,
our souls in sync with sparkling stars,
our hearts filled with citrus petals
and certainty

but, tears fall and yesterdays fade
and even a hope like ours
can be damaged by time

the light was all I wished for you
so I took your demons and gave you my shine

(use it to stay warm on haunting nights)

you and me,
we were obsessed with catastrophe,
chasing waves of destruction
because maybe it'd make us feel
   s o m e t h i n g

but, I got tired of the running
and the late nights
and the false highs
because the lows still came
they still called out my name

and, now
I just want to save you the pain
of the fall
because trust me,
the crash isn't worth the climb

(*and chaos doesn't ease the ache*)

those nights ate away at us,
left us with scars that we pretend don't exist,
swirling memories etched into fragile hearts,
darkness in the gardens
where light used to thrive

we keep looking for a way back in,
the very cracks that could save us
threatening to crumble before our eyes

(*those sacred flaws will lead us home*)

ashley jane

I watched you drowning
in darkness and doubts,
stress pressing
against your chest,
the fire in your heart
reduced to smoke

I saw you struggle
to move on,
your own worries
stacked and arranged
in a makeshift cage,
creating a personal prison
as you held too tightly
to the very thoughts
that left you trapped

all I wanted to do
was help you find
a way out

(*all I wanted to do was set you free*)

The Mums Are Filled With Melancholy

your absence dwells in every pause
of a heart that beats out of tune,
undone by a loss that came much too soon

and there is a soul-stabbing pain
whenever someone says your name

we move in slow motion,
worn down by the ache
and broken wings
that just can't bear to fly

(it hurts too much to say goodbye)

(we miss you, K)

I watch her

in these silent moments,
a wildflower caged within her,
a restless soul
dying to be someone else,
tangled up in solitude,
and I can tell
she has forgotten how to bloom

she is struggling to breathe
in a world too cold,
in an ocean too deep
she is trapped
in this mental captivity

she can't see
that she already has the key
but, she will find the strength

(*the garden in her heart will thrive*)

I see you wasting away,
pennies ill-spent
on wishing wells and broken spells,
caught up in hollow words
spilled from lying lips
you keep chasing love
in all the WRONG places,
searching for some elusive muse to hold you
when the only arms you need
are your own

(*home is your own heart, babe*)

there are secrets
buried behind those cynical eyes of yours,
hallways painted in colors
of darkness and shadow
like tangled nights that we can't unravel

and so many rooms
decorated in crushing images
and cold truths

I see you bare those teeth
anytime I get too close
but there are locks on those doors
that neither of us knows how to decode
and you've got too many ghosts
that vow to protect and serve

(all those skeletons in your closet
 will remain unheard)

dear girl,
I see you there,
feasting on empty words
that spill from foreign tongues,
on feelings living in a rib cage
made from hollow bones

that isn't your home,
not anymore
you cannot keep worshipping a heart
that no longer exists,
and you cannot conjure love from emptiness

so pack up those brittle pieces,
reassemble the broken shards
and please, sweet girl, forget the scars

(you'll find a new home to display your art)

you are dancing
in the rain,
the magic in the music,
the melody echoing from the mountains

you once held the power
of blue skies
behind your gorgeous eyes

but, lately
I watch tornados form
beneath your skin,
the kind created by loss and pain
and made to tear down walls

this storm will pass though,
and you will be the one
capable of breaking hearts
instead of always fighting
not to have yours broken

(you'll be the fire that burns from love)

The Mums Are Filled With Melancholy

the color blue makes me think of you,
of us,
the way we swallow our sorrows,
sipping on sadness
that we do nothing to change

I was never good at love
I like to mix it with angst,
and you keep your emotions
too tightly contained

so, we wallow in this wasteland of doubt,
never searching for a way out,
our regrets drowned
in each shot of whiskey
we down

(*lose the drink and come with me*)

listen
to her heart beat
in shades of broken and bittersweet

— DARK — LIGHT — DARK — LIGHT —

she tries to steady it,
but I hear how it builds
with each breath
and I know this pain,
its echoing ache,
the cold touch of its fingers
around fragile bones

(the same pressing panic
        once made my throat its home)

The Mums Are Filled With Melancholy

we were always so good at running,
trading morning glories for lavender nights,
whiskey sunsets for a tequila sunrise
in a misguided attempt
to save others from us

we made a new home
out of back seats
and bar stools
and blue highways,
always one breath away
from being convinced
that maybe
(just maybe)
we could stay

but, we were never
meant for one place
our hearts are too much like wild horses

(*running is in our veins*)

she is terrified of connection,
the pressure it brings,
of arms that reach out
and mouths that preach hope,
her time better spent chasing after insanity,
making an escape on some midnight train,
only breaking ground
in paper towns with no name
where honesty doesn't spill
quite so freely,
and love is a four letter word
no one dares speak

(*an emotion that shall not be named*)

The Mums Are Filled With Melancholy

she hears the way
your heart beats,
feels the ache
deep within your bones
she watches you,
the way you blanket yourself
in sweet ruin
and let tears stain your cheeks
she sees your indecision
she knows what it feels like

you are scarcely breathing,
but she refuses to let go

(*because she knows*)

midnight chimes
on the old clock in the hallway,
and I watch you
spinning,
those tumultuous thoughts
turning tricks in your mind,
fluid truths and liquid lies
racing through your veins

I need you to breathe

you barely sleep
and wake up shaking
dawn's light and the summer breeze
rush through the window
to kiss your skin
as if they didn't know
that only winter lives there now

I need you to breathe

the day moves
in a slow-sludge-slink
and you sink
a little lower,
the cold settling deep
within your bones

I need you to breathe

you're hidden underneath the blankets
while the dark
does its lazy stretch across the sky,
its fingers untying the last strings of light
and I am still here,
waiting
waiting
waiting
watching for your chest to rise

(*I NEED you to breathe*)

you keep saying
that your kingdom caved,
that all you loved was washed away,
but there are worlds
on the other side of your walls,
and you are losing time,
waiting on your heart to re-knit,
hoping all the pieces fall back into place
I want you
to bloom
to bleed
to burn
to breathe
to become

(*I want you to live*)

The Mums Are Filled With Melancholy

you wield forbidden words,
your grim tales of treason
inked on parchment
and it's killing me,
frantic-heart pounding-anxiety

you say
it's the antidote
for your own version of pain

so, if those stolen slivers of my soul
make you feel whole,
then please
take what you need

(I'll swallow your ache with my own)

the face in the mirror wavers,

unable to hold your gaze
while you catalog every flaw
and search for minute imperfections
(I told you there are none to find)
—

you see shadows
when light is the only thing
that pours from your veins,
all the reasons you matter
safely stored in a cage
(the spark in your heart illuminates the dark)
—

your eyes see distortion,
a tangled mess of proportions,
but your soul knows that the sun lives
beneath your skin,
a shimmering magic that radiates within

and I hope your mind
will learn to see this too

(until then, I'll remind you every day)

The Mums Are Filled With Melancholy

she is too many restless nights
tied up in memory vines,
resisting and falling all over again
she wakes to the cling and clamor,
the noise of old lovers echoing in the quiet
her heart is a ghost train
filled with remnants and hollow remains

(her soul cries out for silence)

her heart doesn't beat

quite the same anymore,
too many run-ins
with a world too fond of tyranny,
too many drive-by tragedies
leaving it full of scars

she doesn't really talk about it anymore,
that ache she holds
far too close to her soul

I suppose she got tired
of reaching out,
desperate for a rope
but finding bits of broken strings
tied to maps that only lead
to cold indifference
and misunderstandings

her mood is muted now,
her mind filled
with monochrome thoughts
that pool together
in shades of shadows and apathy,
all muddied together

The Mums Are Filled With Melancholy

and silence is the only thing
singing in her veins,
its haunting melody
keeping her awake
as she restlessly drifts between
quiet pain and melancholy dreams

(the girl you knew doesn't exist anymore)

ashley jane

she wears nobility like a shield,
the prim and proper posture
holding up a ghost of a girl
she counts beads of amethyst,
but hail marys with purple rosaries
just aren't the same
as the holiness imparted
when you said her name
      just the thought makes it
      hard
            to
                    breathe
she plucks wilted violets
and leaves them on the grave,
tucked in beside your memory
before straightening her face
into a mask of indifference

(you'd never know
    her heart lives in a haunted home)

ashley jane

The Mums Are Filled With Melancholy

I call her haunted,
this ghostly girl
with a heart that barely beats

she is sadness wrapped up
in a broken melody
that gets stuck in my head
the melancholy sound of it
burrows deep
and makes it hard to breathe

(but, I cannot stop listening)

ashley jane

pain held close,
braced by brittle bones,
an ache locked away in a fragile cage

it was yours once,
but I've made it my own

(*I took it from you so you could breathe*)

The Mums Are Filled With Melancholy

I knew I'd like you the moment we met,
all that starlight in your veins
calling my name

you still hold the hand
of everyone you've ever known,
watching over their hearts
while you stand guard

I always put you on a pedestal
because that is where you said I should be

but, my soul has never been as sure as yours,
my back too weak to support
all those totems and pillars
that you single handedly carry

you are so busy ensuring
no one else's walls collapse

but, what about yours?

(who keeps the dam within you from breaking?)

she is crying,
the choked up-can't breathe-drowning
kind of crying
and I'm here, but not really
not the here she needs,
not there beside her,
holding her up
while her world
comes tumbling down

I am miles away,
and this is one pain
where I cannot say,
"I know"
because I don't

I tell her to breathe
because that's what she needs

in truth, I stopped breathing
when the phone rang,
when the screen showed her name
because somewhere inside me
I knew
I just knew
this wasn't like other calls

The Mums Are Filled With Melancholy

I knew that she was sinking
beneath the weight
of all those worries
she carried so strongly
on her back

I knew that she was one step away
from being pulled under,
and I was the one she chose
as a lifeline

(I'll save her even if I can't save myself)

him,
the lonely stranger
with the smoke stained smile
and sad lines etched into his face,
a tired toska uncontained

(his melancholia beckons from the shadows)

you've always been so strong-willed,
never split in your decisions,
always so stubbornly sure
(I think it's the Taurus in you)

you never hesitate,
so determined to succeed,
no wasting time on whispered dreams,
so focused on growing up,
on walking your own path
(there are times you're too much like me)

I hope one day you'll realize
that mistakes can be MAGIC
you were born to fly,
but there are infinite ways
to reach a destination

(I want you to explore each and every one)

I watched you falling,
no wings to fly,
gravity pulling
and your eyes shut tight,
a monsoon of melancholy
flooding your somber heart,
all secluded away in the quiet
    and I just wanted you to know
    that you're never alone

when misty memories
weave worry inside your mind,
foggy fear and doubt
leaving no way out
    I'll never leave you behind

let me take your hand
and together, we'll wait

(*soon, the dawn will break*)

ashley jane

The Mums Are Filled With Melancholy

*You can't see your shadows
when you're facing the sun*

- Matt Shirley

despite
what it seems,
you are stronger
than those sad goodbyes
that crash like waves
against your heart

(you are braver than those wild currents
                          trying to pull you out to sea)

she is this sweet beauty,
encased in mist,
with an air of ethereal ghostliness,
a mortal girl with a spirit's soul

(she is sadness encased in hope)

ashley jane

for so long,
we ran after the rush
we chased lust and called it living,
school day crushes
traded for one night stands
until we finally realized
that we need to love ourselves
if we want to survive

(*only* [*self*] *love will save us*)

The Mums Are Filled With Melancholy

we have spent decades
mending ourselves with little journals
filled with sepia stained pages,
marked by tears and age
and the frantic release
of words strung together
in a struggle to purge the ache
and replace it
with a – TEMPORARY – feeling of relief

(some days, temporary is enough)

ashley jane

we used to chase hope
under an empire of lights,
the silver flicker of falling stars
illuminating the night

but, all the stars have fallen,
and each wish has been made

our minds have become clouded
as we've watched the day fade

we found no mercy in the darkness,
no sweet reprieve in sight

but, there is still something
burning within us

(we'll use that to repaint the sky)

uncertainty
clings to us
like a second skin

a ghostly glimmer
of the demons within

an ocean of worries
behind our eyes

(*but, we can still turn the tide*)

ashley jane

things we are good at:

the

way

we

run

until

distance

tears

away

at

us

The Mums Are Filled With Melancholy

things we need to be better at:

the
way
we
search
the
shadows
for
sparks
of
light

we were all chips and cracks,
bits of sadly shattered pieces scattered about
but there was beauty in our brokenness
and in the way our spirits
lingered in the shards
we let love bloom in the fault lines,
watched hope transform every flaw
like kintsugi magic

(*we were reborn from our scars*)

The Mums Are Filled With Melancholy

she wrings her hands,
cold fingers aching
from hours spent
writing away the wrongs,
caught up in the fragility
and the futility of it all,
knowing that hope
is the rope she'll hang by

yet, you'll find her...
running back
for more every single time

you'll find her
watching out the window,
listening to the way
the rain speaks
through the storm,
trusting it will
wash away the pain
and the darkness will
weep tears of light
once more

(you'll find her waiting for the sun)

ashley jane

she is a dangerous combination,
a bittersweet soul
with a heart that believes

she likes the way the willow weeps
and how the spider mums
bloom best in the shade

she waits for you there,
with them,
within the kissing shadows,
hoping your hands can hold
all her melancholy hope

(*hoping your light will be her home*)

she is ghost and goddess,
a wild whisper of something ethereal,
a holy haunting
that dances in your mind

she will prove
that even the shadows
are filled with bits of light

(*just give her time*)

I chase after the pretty abandoned,
search for the lost
trying to make it through the woods
the winter can be cold,
and the nights can get rough

but I just want to watch them bloom
I must have flowers,
always, always, always

so, I am clinging to hope
in a forest of pine needles and promises,
turning remnants of shadows
into petals of light

(*they make for beautiful sunlit blossoms*)

The Mums Are Filled With Melancholy

I looked for peace behind the veil,
searched for the perfect shelter for my soul
on days when the darkness comes calling
and nights where depression looms
with its black magic and words of illusion,
so determined to sway
my already conflicted mind
and steal away what remains
of my inner strength

(I refuse to let the monsters get the best of me)

truth and pain

lay pressed,
locked away in this cage
in my chest

I nestled them in beside
every
breath.
stealing.
word.
every lie
every promise
every betrayal
every love

I let them break me and make me,
let them crush my spirit,
let them heal my soul

I turned them into strength,
but only after letting them
be my weakness

I still know their sound,
and it echoes in my head
on long nights
when sleep doesn't come

The Mums Are Filled With Melancholy

the way they push
against my ribs still stings
and, I can still feel them
racing to catch up with my heart

but, I was born
of bolder things,
better things,
beautiful things

I will never let them
leave me gasping

(*I will never let them swallow me whole*)

you held my hand
while the ache held my heart,
kept me warm while the cold
ran rampant in my veins
I was one break away from falling apart,
but you took my pain

(thank you for bringing me back from the brink)

ashley jane

I remember that summer,
the way we embraced our freedom,
how it tasted like strawberry hill
and our wildest dreams
we passed around bottles of Boone's Farm
and crashed on the pier beneath the stars
we were sunny smiles wrapped up
in moonlight and honeysuckle,
our wild hearts filled
with recklessness and hope

if only we'd known...

we grew older
dusk has settled into our bones,
and the dark has brushed against our souls
more than we care to admit
the pain in our words is authentic
we bleed in shades of sadness,
and we've been touched by far too much grief
but we keep moving
because it's all we know how to do

(*maybe our wild hearts still hold a little hope*)

her destiny fades
in the hands of fickle fate,
her luck absent,
tucked away
without a trace,
heart beats quicken,
a pulse like raindrops
and she's drowning in them
her white knuckle grip
on sanity
begins to slip,
a compelling urge
to run away
from the hurt now creeping
through her veins
as the half moon hangs,
a cynical sliver
beyond the fog

(but it'll do to light her way)

darkness falls
in tune with her heart,
staccato tones
that collide with the silence
and dance through the quiet

she lingers,
a nightingale wrapped
in the beauty of shadows,
bringing the light
to get you through until dawn

(*listen to her healing song*)

ashley jane

the pulse
of the universe
beats softly
in her chest

the melancholy song
of a heart that aches
to rest

(*it's calling out to you*)

she speaks
in stream of consciousness,
words flooding the silence,
the birth of darkness and doubt
spilling out from her soul
she is almost everywhere,
and nowhere,
holding onto a fear that won't let her go
as she rambles on
about the fight
between truth and lies,
disbelief shining out from jaded eyes
but, if you look close
you'll see that her heart
still tenuously clings to hope

(*she refuses to let go*)

we hide ourselves
behind tall walls
and guarded hearts
we camouflage ourselves in apathy
and sleep under blankets of secrets
we do everything we can
to keep people out,
to push people away,
so afraid of allowing anyone
to see the pain we conceal

(but, the healers still find a way)

The Mums Are Filled With Melancholy

we cut the rope
made of darling daisy chains,
exhaled the barbed fear thorns in our way
we were drowning in dirt and doubt,
clamoring towards the surface,
struggling to find a way out
but, these flowers are breaking
like waves against our skin,
a cleansing rush of soft petals and promises
we inhale the soft scent of forgiveness

(our blossoming hearts can be whole again)

I think
we try too hard
to hide from the light,
naively believing
we are home within the darkness

but these shadows are not all ours

we are more than broken hearts
and brittle bones

(*maybe the light is where we belong*)

bittersweet,
this melody of ours,
the way we speak
of rewriting destiny

we're calling out
beneath the icy sting,
chasing after dewdrops
and daydreams,
and this elusive thing called
h o m e
our voices raised
in a mournful song
that pierces the fog
of these faded nights
so our open eyes
can find strength in the tides

(we sing, and the waves bring us home)

too many
sleep with reason,
becoming slaves to logic
and perfect control,
failing to see
the beauty found
in *a b a n d o n*

(there is freedom in letting go)

The Mums Are Filled With Melancholy

we beg for peace
between moments
of war and sin,
aching for hope
in a love-starved land

(let's welcome the light in)

ashley jane

fast forward a few years,
and you'll hear
about the poets
whose ghosts rose
from these ethereal walls,
having lingered in old corners
and dusty shelves
filled with books
that haven't been read enough
and pictures that no one appreciates

(*don't let the poetry fade away*)

daylight slips
behind the hanging moon,
and we watch
the shadows settle,
our greedy hearts hungry
for a different kind of change

(*thoughts and prayers*)

the world we knew

is nothing more
than a gasp in the past

a quick inhale of truth
before the lies settled in

now, the party's over,
and the story we wrote
of love
and good
is just a letter to the ocean,
sinking somewhere in the deep
with the fading remnants of humanity
and our restless, recurring dreams
of change

(yet, I still cling to the hope in my veins)

ashley jane

The Mums Are Filled With Melancholy

She whispered wishes
to the rose petals,
but it was always
the mums that answered

(her spring heart is no match
for her autumn soul)

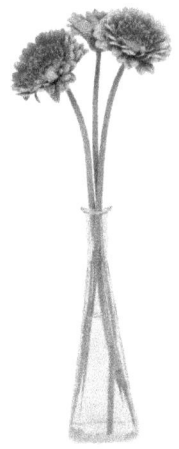

ashley jane

Acknowledgements

To my other half who provides endless support and encourages me to pursue this dream (and also provides his amazing typing skills and delicious popcorn). I would be lost without you. Love you.

To my family who cheer me on and root for my success. To the friends I've known forever, thank you for having my back and reminding me to never give up. I am so lucky to have you guys in my corner. Thank you. I love you all.

To my beautifully talented cousin, Nadiya. Your art skills have always amazed me, and I am so glad you agreed to join me on this journey.

Chels, Matt, Alfa, Gypsy, and Emma – thanks for allowing me to use your beautiful quotes in my book. Chelsea, Matt, Alfa, Nicole, Jamie – thank you for the feedback, the constructive criticism, the amazing assistance. You are all such incredible people, and I am so blessed to call you all friends.

To the many social media folks and fans I've had the opportunity to meet this past year. You are all amazing, and I am so lucky to have you in my corner.

To my fellow readers, writers and prompters, thank you for inspiring me in so many ways. I am lucky to be part of such a fantastic community.

To everyone who bought my first book of poetry, Love, Lies and Lullabies, and those who buy this one, it means so much to me to know my words ended up in appreciative hands. Thank you for your endless support!

About the Author

Ashley writes with a wisdom and experience born of having lived with a very real sense of the fragility of life. A lupus defeater since her early teens, she has not only overcome that sometimes debilitating reality, but she has learnt to wield hope as a shield. That sense of hope shines, even when reading the darker themes she often chooses explore. Themes she displays an innate and uncanny understanding of, as she leads us into places of such rich, eloquent imagery they become real.

And in this, her second collection of poetics, that sense of hope blossoms as she explores the subject of melancholy. A melancholy that, at times, seems so incredibly palpable one can almost see the petals of chrysanthemums falling like tears; but the tears are lit with hope. While her first book explored love, this one explores life!

A long time contributor of micro-poetry, she voluntarily runs a number of inspirational social media based prompts and writing pages to help others in their creative endeavours.

Ashley lives with her husband, extended family and a rather monkey like Shadow-cat, in Alabama, US...and it is from there that we feel and hear the whispers of her words that breathe between night and day.

One could not ask for a more kind, loving and supportive friend.

Matt
aseawords

Other books by this Author:

Love, Lies and Lullabies
Ashley Jane

Love. Lies and Lullabies

Find Me on Social Media

Web: www.breathwords.com

Facebook: www.facebook.com/breathwords

Instagram: @breathwords

Twitter: @breathwords

Pinterest: www.pinterest.com/breathwordspoems

Tumblr: @breathwords

Vero: @breathwords

Mirakee: @breathwords

Lettrs: @breathwords

Poetizer: Ashley Jane (breathwords)

For more words by the amazing writers
featured on the dividers,
check out the following:

Alfa Holden
Instagram: @alfa.poet
Facebook: @alfawrites
Alfapoet.com

Chelsea Lopez
Instagram: @chelseainchicago
chelsearaelopez@gmail.com

Emma Blas
Instagram: @phoenixrisespoetry

Gypsy Mercer
Instagram: mercergypsy
Facebook: @gypsysong
GypsyMercer.com

Matt Shirley
Instagram: @aseawords
Twitter: @a_sea_of_words

ashley jane

Cover Art by:
Nadiya El-Sharkawy

Additional Art and Photography by:
Annie Spratt
Jerry Kiesewetter
Doug Kelley
Irina Iriser
Eva Waardenburg
Rikki Austen
Wendy Scofield
Luis Villasmil
Pixabay

www.ingramcontent.com/pod-product-compliance
Lightning Source LLC
Chambersburg PA
CBHW071159070526
44584CB00019B/2846